Adapted Reading and Study

Inside Earth

PRENTICE HALL **Science** Explorer

PEARSON

Prentice
Hall

Boston, Massachusetts
Upper Saddle River, New Jersey

ISBN 0-13-166544-8
2 3 4 5 6 7 8 9 10   09 08 07 06 05

Inside Earth

Chapter 1 Plate Tectonics

Chapter 2 Earthquakes

Chapter 3 Volcanoes

Chapter 4 Minerals

Chapter 5 Rocks

Plate Tectonics

Earth's Interior (pages 6–13)

Exploring Inside Earth (pages 7–8)

Key Concept: **Geologists have used two main types of evidence to learn about Earth's interior: direct evidence from rock samples and indirect evidence from seismic waves.**

- Scientists cannot travel inside Earth to explore it. So scientists must learn about Earth's interior, or inside, in other ways.

- Scientists use drills to get rock samples from inside Earth. The rock samples help scientists learn what conditions were like inside Earth when the rocks formed.

- Scientists study how seismic waves travel through Earth. **Seismic** (SYZ mik) **waves** are waves made by earthquakes. Seismic waves show that Earth is made up of layers like an onion.

Answer the following questions. Use your textbook and the ideas above.

1. Circle the letter of a way that scientists can learn about Earth's interior.
   a. travel inside Earth and explore it directly
   b. study rock samples from inside Earth
   c. peel away Earth's layers like an onion

2. Is the following sentence true or false? Earth is made up of layers. _____

Name _____ Date _____ Class _____

A Journey to the Center of Earth (page 9)

Key Concept: **The three main layers of Earth are the crust, the mantle, and the core. These layers vary greatly in size, composition, temperature, and pressure.**

- Earth has three main layers. The crust is the outside layer. The mantle is the middle layer. The core is the inside layer.

- Temperature increases from the crust to the core. It is very hot inside Earth. One reason it is so hot is that some substances inside Earth give off energy.

- Pressure also increases from the crust to the core. **Pressure** is caused by a force pressing on an area. There is great pressure inside Earth because of all the rock pressing down from above.

Answer the following questions. Use your textbook and the ideas above.

3. Fill in the blanks in the diagram about Earth's layers.

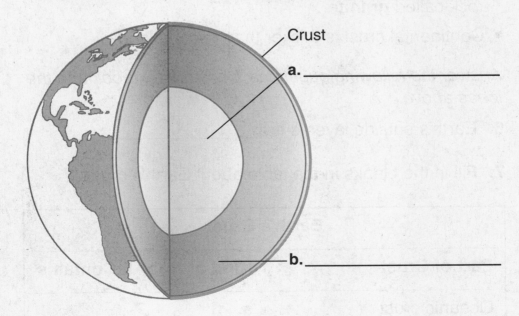

Crust

a. _____

b. _____

Plate Tectonics

4. Is the following sentence true or false? Earth's temperature decreases from the crust to the core.

_____

5. The layer of Earth that is under the greatest pressure is the _____.

The Crust (page 10)

Key Concept: **The crust is a layer of solid rock that includes both dry land and the ocean floor.**

- The **crust** is a layer of rock that forms Earth's outer skin. The crust is Earth's thinnest layer. It is only 5 to 70 kilometers thick.

- The crust that makes up the ocean floors is called oceanic crust. Oceanic crust is made mostly of a rock called **basalt** (buh SAWLT).

- The crust that makes up the continents is called continental crust. Continental crust is made mostly of a rock called **granite**.

- Continental crust is thicker than oceanic crust.

Answer the following questions. Use your textbook and the ideas above.

6. Earth's outside layer is the _____.

7. Fill in the blanks in the table about Earth's crust.

Earth's Crust	
Part of Crust	**Kind of Rock It Contains**
Oceanic crust	a. _____
b. _____	granite

Plate Tectonics

8. Is the following sentence true or false? Oceanic crust is thicker than continental crust. _____

The Mantle (page 11)

Key Concept: **Earth's mantle is made up of rock that is very hot, but solid. Scientists divide the mantle into layers based on the physical characteristics of those layers. Overall, the mantle is nearly 3,000 kilometers thick.**

- The **mantle** is the layer below the crust. The mantle is Earth's thickest layer. The mantle has three layers.

- The top layer of the mantle, along with the crust, is the **lithosphere** (LITH uh sfeer). The top layer of the mantle is hard rock.

- The middle layer of the mantle is the **asthenosphere** (as THEN uh sfeer). The middle layer is soft rock, like hot road tar.

- The bottom layer of the mantle is called the lower mantle. It is also hard rock.

Answer the following questions. Use your textbook and the ideas above.

9. Circle the letter of each sentence that is true about the mantle.
   a. The mantle is the layer below the crust.
   b. The mantle is Earth's thinnest layer.
   c. The lower mantle is made of hard rock.

10. Read the words in the box. In each sentence below, fill in one of the words.

lithosphere	crust	asthenosphere

a. The top layer of the mantle is part of the

_____.

b. The layer of the mantle that is made of soft rock is

the _____.

The Core (pages 12–13)

Key Concept: **The core is made mostly of the metals iron and nickel. It consists of two parts—a liquid outer core and a solid inner core.**

* The **core** is Earth's inside layer. The core has two layers: the outer core and the inner core.

* The **outer core** is made of liquid metal. The liquid metal flows in currents. The currents make Earth act like a giant magnet, with north and south poles that attract iron.

* The **inner core** is made of solid metal. The inner core is solid because it is under so much pressure.

Answer the following questions. Use your textbook and the ideas above.

11. Circle the letter of each sentence that is true about Earth's core.

a. The core is made mostly of iron and nickel.

b. The core is Earth's inside layer.

c. The core is a giant magnet.

12. Fill in the blanks in the concept map about Earth's core.

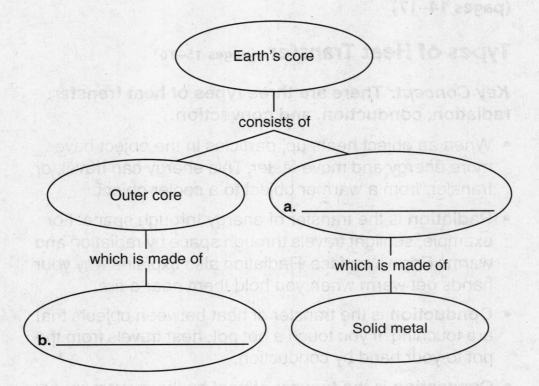

13. Is the following sentence true or false? Earth acts like a giant magnet because of currents in the outer core.

_____

Plate Tectonics

Convection and the Mantle
(pages 14–17)

Types of Heat Transfer (pages 15–16)

Key Concept: **There are three types of heat transfer: radiation, conduction, and convection.**

- When an object heats up, particles in the object have more energy and move faster. This energy can travel, or transfer, from a warmer object to a cooler object.

- **Radiation** is the transfer of energy through space. For example, sunlight travels through space by radiation and warms Earth's surface. Radiation also explains why your hands get warm when you hold them near a fire.

- **Conduction** is the transfer of heat between objects that are touching. If you touch a hot pot, heat travels from the pot to your hand by conduction.

- **Convection** is the transfer of heat by the movement of particles in fluids such as water. Moving particles transfer heat throughout the fluid.

Answer the following questions. Use your textbook and the ideas above.

1. The kind of heat transfer that warms Earth's surface on a sunny day is _____.

2. Circle the letter of an example of conduction.
   a. A sidewalk gets hot on a sunny day.
   b. A pot gets hot on a stove.
   c. A bench gets hot near a campfire.

3. The transfer of heat by the movement of particles in fluids is _____.

Convection Currents (page 16)

Key Concept: **Heating and cooling of a fluid, changes in the fluid's density, and the force of gravity combine to set convection currents in motion.**

- Remember, convection is the transfer of heat by the movement of particles in fluids. This movement of particles is called a **convection current**.

- A convection current starts when there are differences in temperature and density in a fluid. **Density** is the amount of mass in a given volume of a substance. A high-density substance feels heavy for its size.

- Suppose you put a pot of soup on a stove. The soup at the bottom of the pot gets warm first. Because it is warmer, the soup at the bottom is less dense than the cooler soup above it. So the warmer soup rises. At the same time, the cooler, denser soup sinks to the bottom of the pot.

- The cooler soup now at the bottom gets warmer, and the process repeats. A constant flow of particles begins. Warmer soup keeps rising, and cooler soup keeps sinking. This movement of particles transfers heat throughout the soup.

Answer the following questions. Use your textbook and the ideas above.

4. Circle the set of arrows that shows how a convection current flows through the liquid in the pot.

Plate Tectonics

5. Is the following sentence true or false? A convection current starts when there are differences in temperature and volume in a fluid. _____

Convection Currents in Earth (page 17)

Key Concept: **Heat from the core and the mantle itself causes convection currents in the mantle.**

- The heat inside Earth causes convection currents in the mantle and outer core.

- Convection currents inside Earth are like convection currents in a pot of soup. Hot materials at the bottom rise to the top. Cooler materials at the top sink to the bottom.

- Convection currents in the mantle move very slowly. This is because the mantle is made of solid rock.

- Remember, Earth is like a giant magnet because of currents in the outer core. Those currents are convection currents.

Answer the following questions. Use your textbook and the ideas above.

6. The layers of Earth that have convection currents are

the mantle and _____.

7. Circle the letter of the sentence that correctly describes how convection currents move inside Earth.
   a. Hot materials rise, while cooler materials sink.
   b. Hot materials sink, while cooler materials rise.
   c. Hot materials move up or down, while cooler materials move sideways.

Plate Tectonics

Drifting Continents (pages 18–22)

Continental Drift (pages 19–21)

Key Concept: **Alfred Wegener's hypothesis was that all the continents were once joined together in a single landmass and have since drifted apart. Wegener gathered evidence from different scientific fields to support his ideas about continental drift. He studied land features, fossils, and evidence of climate change.**

- Some continents are shaped like puzzle pieces. For example, the west side of Africa and the east side of South America look like matching puzzle pieces.

- Scientist Alfred Wegener (VAY guh nur) tried to explain why continents are shaped this way.

- Wegener thought that Earth had one big continent about 300 million years ago. The big continent broke into smaller pieces and formed smaller continents. The continents slowly drifted apart. Wegener called this **continental drift**.

- Evidence shows that continental drift really happened. Mountain ranges in Africa and South America line up as if they were once part of the same mountain range. Other evidence shows that continents once had different climates. This could happen if continents had drifted.

Answer the following questions. Use your textbook and the ideas above.

1. Wegener called the slow movement of continents

   _____.

Plate Tectonics

2. Circle the letter of the drawing that shows how Wegener thought South America and Africa were once joined as part of a single, giant continent.

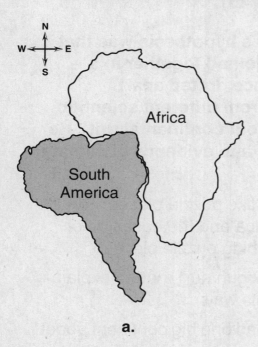

a.

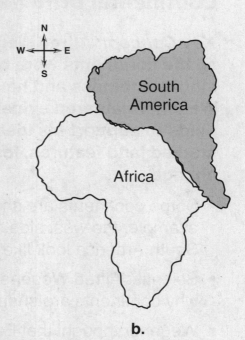

b.

3. Circle the letter of evidence that supports Wegener's idea of continental drift.

   a. Mountain ranges on different continents line up.

   b. Evidence shows that climates have not changed.

   c. Old maps show that Earth had a single, giant continent about 3,000 years ago.

Plate Tectonics

Wegener's Hypothesis Rejected (page 22)

Key Concept: **Unfortunately, Wegener could not provide a satisfactory explanation for the force that pushes or pulls the continents.**

- Wegener could not explain what causes continental drift. So most other scientists of his time thought that he was wrong.

- Wegener used his idea of continental drift to explain how mountains form. Wegener thought mountains form because drifting continents bump into each other. When this happens, edges of the continents crumple. The crumpled edges form mountains.

Answer the following questions. Use your textbook and the ideas above.

4. Is the following sentence true or false? Wegener's ideas were accepted by most other scientists of

   his time. _____

5. Circle the letter of the sentence that describes how Wegener thought mountains form.
   a. Earth slowly cools and shrinks.
   b. Continents drift apart.
   c. Continents bump into each other.

Plate Tectonics

Sea-Floor Spreading (pages 23–29)

Mid-Ocean Ridges (page 24)

Key Concept: **Mid-ocean ridges lie beneath Earth's oceans.**

- Since the mid-1900s, scientists have used sonar to study the ocean floor. **Sonar** is a device that bounces sound waves off underwater objects. The longer it takes the sound waves to bounce back, the farther away the objects are.

- Using sonar, scientists found long mountain ranges on the ocean floors. Scientists call the mountain ranges **mid-ocean ridges**. Mid-ocean ridges run through the middle of all oceans.

- In a few places, mid-ocean ridges poke above the surface and form islands. Iceland is the top of a mid-ocean ridge in the North Atlantic Ocean.

Answer the following questions. Use your textbook and the ideas above.

1. Is the following sentence true or false? Scientists use sound waves to study the ocean floor. _____

2. Circle the letter of each sentence that is true about mid-ocean ridges.
   a. Mid-ocean ridges are mountain ranges on the ocean floor.
   b. Mid-ocean ridges sometimes form islands.
   c. Mid-ocean ridges are found only in the Atlantic Ocean.

What Is Sea-Floor Spreading? (page 25)

Key Concept: In sea-floor spreading, the sea floor spreads apart along both sides of a mid-ocean ridge as new crust is added. As a result, the ocean floors move like conveyor belts, carrying the continents along with them.

- **Sea-floor spreading** is a process that slowly adds new rock to the ocean floors. Scientist Harry Hess came up with the idea of sea-floor spreading in 1960.

- Here is how sea-floor spreading works. In the center of a mid-ocean ridge, melted rock pushes up through cracks in the ocean floor. The melted rock pushes older, solid rock away from both sides of the ridge. The melted rock cools and forms new solid rock at the center of the ridge.

- This process keeps repeating. Slowly, the ocean floor is pushed farther and farther away from both sides of the mid-ocean ridge. At the same time, new rock keeps adding to the ocean floor in the center of the ridge.

Answer the following questions. Use your textbook and the ideas above.

3. The process that slowly adds new rock to the ocean

   floors is called _____.

4. Circle the letter of each sentence that is true about sea-floor spreading.
   a. Harry Hess came up with the idea of sea-floor spreading.
   b. Sea-floor spreading happens at mid-ocean ridges.
   c. In sea-floor spreading, the ocean floor is pushed aside by hard rock from the core.

5. The diagram shows sea-floor spreading. Circle the letter of the two arrows that show the directions in which the sea floor is spreading.

   a. A and B   **b.** A and C   **c.** B and C

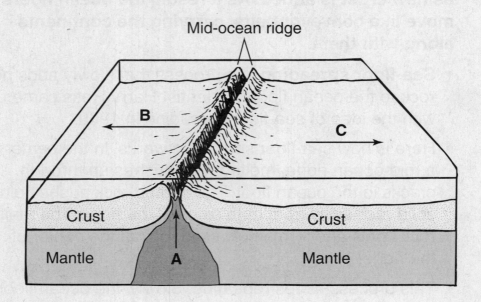

Evidence for Sea-Floor Spreading (pages 26–27)

Key Concept: **Several types of evidence supported Hess's theory of sea-floor spreading: eruptions of molten material, magnetic stripes in the rock of the ocean floor, and the ages of the rocks themselves.**

- In the 1960s, scientists tried to find evidence for sea-floor spreading.

- Scientists used a submarine to get rocks from a mid-ocean ridge. The rocks showed that melted rock had hardened again and again along the ridge.

- Scientists used a drill to get rocks from below the ocean floor. Rocks closest to a mid-ocean ridge were the newest. Rocks farthest from a mid-ocean ridge were the oldest.

- From evidence such as this, scientists knew that sea-floor spreading really happens.

Plate Tectonics

Answer the following question. Use your textbook and the ideas on page 18.

6. Circle the letter of each choice that correctly describes evidence for sea-floor spreading.

   a. Melted rocks have hardened again and again at mid-ocean ridges.

   b. Rocks closest to mid-ocean ridges are the oldest.

   c. Rocks farthest from mid-ocean ridges are the oldest.

Subduction at Trenches (pages 28–29)

***Key Concept:* In a process taking tens of millions of years, part of the ocean floor sinks back into the mantle at deep-ocean trenches.**

- Sea-floor spreading makes the ocean floors get wider. New rock keeps forming at mid-ocean ridges. Old rock keeps getting pushed farther and farther away from both sides of the ridges.

- After millions of years, old rock reaches underwater canyons, called **deep-ocean trenches**. At a deep-ocean trench, the rocky crust of the ocean floor bends downward and sinks into the mantle. This process is called **subduction** (sub DUK shun).

- Sea-floor spreading and subduction work together. They keep the ocean floors moving like conveyor belts in an airport. As new rock is added to the ocean floors, old rock disappears. Overall, the size of the ocean floors does not change very much.

Answer the following questions. Use your textbook and the ideas above.

7. The process in which ocean floors sink into the mantle

   is called _____.

8. Fill in the blanks in the table about changes in the ocean floors.

How the Ocean Floors Change		
Process	**Happens at**	**Makes Ocean Floor**
Sea-floor spreading	mid-ocean ridges	bigger
Subduction	a. _____ _____	b. _____

9. Is the following sentence true or false? Overall, the size of the ocean floor does not change very much.

_____

The Theory of Plate Tectonics (pages 32–36)

How Plates Move (page 33)

Key Concept: **The theory of plate tectonics explains the formation, movement, and subduction of Earth's plates.**

- Earth's surface is broken into many jagged pieces. The surface is like the shell of a hard-boiled egg that has been dropped. The pieces of Earth's surface are called **plates**. Plates carry continents, ocean floors, or both.

- The theory of **plate tectonics** (tek TAHN iks) says that Earth's plates move because of convection currents in the mantle. Currents in the mantle carry plates on Earth's surface, like currents in water carry boats on a river.

- Plates can meet in three different ways. Plates may pull apart, push together, or slide past each other. Wherever plates meet, you usually find volcanoes, mountain ranges, or deep-ocean trenches.

Answer the following questions. Use your textbook and the ideas above.

1. Jagged pieces of Earth's surface are called

   _____.

2. Is the following sentence true or false? Earth's plates carry only the continents. _____

3. Circle the letter of the sentence that states the theory of plate tectonics.

   a. Earth's plates cannot move because they are made of solid rock.

   b. Earth's plates move because of convection currents in the mantle.

   c. Earth's moving plates cause convection currents in the mantle.

Plate Boundaries (pages 34–36)

Key Concept: **There are three kinds of plate boundaries: divergent boundaries, convergent boundaries, and transform boundaries. A different type of plate movement occurs along each type of boundary.**

- A plate boundary is where two plates meet. Faults form along plate boundaries. A **fault** is a break in Earth's crust where blocks of rock have slipped past each other.

- Where two plates move apart, the boundary is called a **divergent** (dy VUR junt) **boundary**. A divergent boundary between two oceanic plates forms a mid-ocean ridge. A divergent boundary between two continental plates forms a deep valley called a **rift valley**.

- Where two plates push together, the boundary is called a **convergent** (kun VUR junt) **boundary**. A convergent boundary between two oceanic plates forms a deep-ocean trench. A convergent boundary between two continental plates forms a mountain range.

- Where two plates slide past each other in opposite directions, the plate boundary is called a **transform boundary**. At a transform boundary, earthquakes may occur.

Name _____ Date _____ Class _____

Plate Tectonics

Answer the following questions. Use your textbook and the ideas on page 22.

4. Read the words in the box. In each sentence below, fill in one of the words.

```
fault      boundary      rift
```

   a. The edges of two plates meet at a plate _____.

   b. A break in Earth's crust where blocks of rock have slipped past each other is a _____.

5. Fill in the blanks in the table about plate boundaries.

Plate Boundaries		
Type of Plate Boundary	**How Plates Move**	**What Forms or Happens**
Divergent boundary	plates move apart	mid-ocean ridges or rift valleys
Convergent boundary	a. _____ _____ _____	deep-ocean trenches or mountain ranges
b. _____ _____	plates slide past each other	earthquakes

Earthquakes

Forces in Earth's Crust

(pages 44–50)

Types of Stress (page 45)

Key Concept: **Tension, compression, and shearing work over millions of years to change the shape and volume of rock.**

- When Earth's plates move, rocks are pushed and pulled. The pushes and pulls are called **stress**.

- Stress adds energy to rocks. Rocks keep storing the energy until they cannot stand any more stress. Then the rocks break or change shape.

- **Tension** is stress that pulls and stretches rocks. Tension makes rocks thinner in the middle. Tension happens when two plates move apart.

- **Compression** is stress that squeezes rocks. Compression makes rocks fold or break. Compression happens when two plates push together.

- **Shearing** is stress that pushes rocks in opposite directions. Shearing makes rocks break, slip apart, or change shape. Shearing happens when two plates slip past each other in opposite directions.

Answer the following questions. Use your textbook and the ideas above.

1. Circle the letter of the choice that describes how stress affects rocks.

   a. Stress adds energy to rocks.

   b. Stress uses up the energy in rocks.

   c. Stress squeezes energy out of rocks.

Earthquakes

2. Read the words in the box. In each sentence below, fill in one of the words.

shearing	compression	stress
folding	tension	

a. Pushes and pulls on rocks are called

_____.

b. Stress that makes rocks fold is called

_____.

c. Stress that stretches rocks is called

_____.

d. Stress that makes rocks slip apart or change

shape is called _____.

3. Fill in the blanks to label the kinds of stress shown.

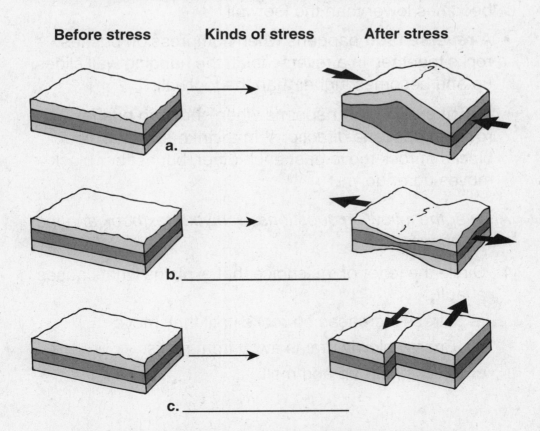

Before stress   **Kinds of stress**   **After stress**

a. _____

b. _____

c. _____

Earthquakes

Earthquakes

Kinds of Faults (pages 46–47)

Key Concept: **Most faults occur along plate boundaries, where the forces of plate motion push or pull the crust so much that the crust breaks. There are three main types of faults: normal faults, reverse faults, and strike-slip faults.**

- A fault is a break in Earth's crust where rocks are under stress.

- In many faults, the fault line is slanted. So the block of rock on one side of the fault is above the block of rock on the other side of the fault. The top block is called the **hanging wall**. The bottom block is called the **footwall**.

- There are three different types of faults: normal faults, reverse faults, and strike-slip faults. Each type is caused by a different kind of stress on rocks.

- A **normal fault** happens when tension pulls rocks apart. In a normal fault, the hanging wall slips down and becomes lower than the footwall.

- A **reverse fault** happens when compression pushes rocks together. In a reverse fault, the hanging wall slides up and becomes higher than the footwall.

- A **strike-slip fault** happens when shearing pushes rocks in opposite directions. In a strike-slip fault, two blocks of rock move past each other, but neither block moves up or down.

Answer the following questions. Use your textbook and the ideas above.

4. Circle the letter of the choice that explains what causes a fault.

   a. Stress increases on rocks until they move.

   b. Energy slowly drains away from rocks.

   c. Rocks heat up and melt.

Earthquakes

5. Fill in the blanks in the table about faults and stresses.

Faults and Stresses	
Kind of Fault	**Type of Stress That Causes Fault**
Normal fault	a. _____
b. _____ _____	compression
c. _____ _____	shearing

6. Fill in the blanks to label the kind of fault shown in each diagram.

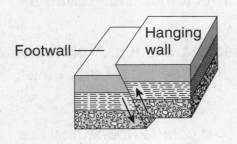

Footwall — Hanging wall

a. _____

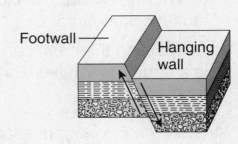

Footwall — Hanging wall

b. _____

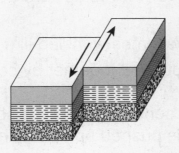

c. _____

Earthquakes

Changing Earth's Surface (pages 48–50)

Key Concept: **Over millions of years, the forces of plate movement can change a flat plain into landforms such as anticlines and synclines, folded mountains, fault-block mountains, and plateaus.**

- Stresses in Earth's crust cause the surface to change. Different stresses cause different changes.

- Compression causes folding. Folding is like a rug getting wrinkled up when it is pushed across the floor.

- Folds that bend upward into ridges are called **anticlines**. Folds that bend downward into valleys are called **synclines**.

- Tension causes stretching. When crust stretches, many normal faults form.

- Sometimes a block of rock moves upward between two normal faults. The block forms a mountain called a fault-block mountain.

- Stresses in the crust can also form plateaus. A **plateau** is a large area of flat land that has been lifted up above sea level.

Answer the following questions. Use your textbook and the ideas above.

7. Circle the letter of the sentence that describes how a fault-block mountain forms.

   a. A block of rock moves upward between two normal faults.

   b. The crust becomes wrinkled like a rug.

   c. Rocks are pushed together by compression.

8. Is the following sentence true or false? A plateau forms when flat land is pushed up above the surrounding land. _____

Name _____ Date _____ Class _____

Earthquakes

9. Circle the letter of the stress that causes Earth's
   surface to look like the surface in the diagram below.
   a. tension
   b. compression
   c. shearing

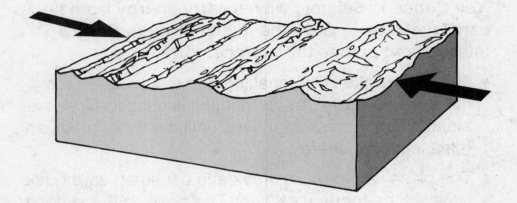

Earthquakes and Seismic Waves (pages 51–57)

Types of Seismic Waves (pages 52–53)

Key Concept: **Seismic waves carry energy from an earthquake away from the focus, through Earth's interior, and across the surface.**

- An **earthquake** is the shaking that results when rocks move inside Earth. An earthquake is caused by stress along a fault. Stress increases until the rocks break and release stored energy.

- The place where rocks break and cause an earthquake is called the **focus** (FOH kus). The point on the surface directly above the focus is called the **epicenter** (EP uh sen tur).

- Earthquakes cause waves, called seismic waves, to travel through Earth. Seismic waves carry the energy released by the rocks. There are three kinds of seismic waves: P waves, S waves, and surface waves.

- **P waves** move rocks back and forth, like a wave passing through a spring toy when you push in the coils. P waves are the fastest seismic waves.

- **S waves** move rocks up and down, like a wave passing through a rope when you flick it. S waves travel more slowly than P waves but do more damage.

- **Surface waves** are combined P and S waves that travel along Earth's surface. Surface waves are the slowest seismic waves. They also do a lot of damage.

Answer the following questions. Use your textbook and the ideas above.

1. When the ground shakes because rocks have moved inside Earth, it is called a(an) _____.

2. Label the circles in the Venn diagram to show which circle describes P waves and which circle describes S waves.

a. _____   b. _____

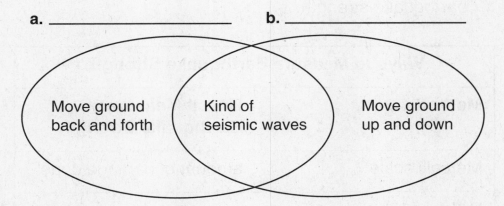

Move ground back and forth

Kind of seismic waves

Move ground up and down

3. Circle the letter of the kind of seismic waves that are the slowest.
   a. P waves
   b. S waves
   c. surface waves

Measuring Earthquakes (pages 54–56)

Key Concept: **Three commonly used methods of measuring earthquakes are the Mercalli scale, the Richter scale, and the moment magnitude scale.**

- The **Mercalli scale** is based on the amount of damage an earthquake does. For example, a weak earthquake only rattles dishes. A strong earthquake can destroy buildings.

- The **Richter scale** is based on the size of the seismic waves. A stronger earthquake makes bigger seismic waves. An instrument called a **seismograph** measures the size of seismic waves.

- The **moment magnitude scale** is based on the amount of energy an earthquake releases. The amount of energy is based on many things, including the size of the seismic waves.

Name _____ Date _____ Class _____

Earthquakes

Answer the following questions. Use your textbook and the ideas on page 31.

4. Fill in the blanks in the table about ways to measure earthquake strength.

Ways to Measure Earthquake Strength	
Method	**How It Measures Earthquake Strength**
Mercalli scale	amount of damage done
Richter scale	**a.** _____ _____
b. _____ _____	amount of energy released

5. An instrument that measures the size of seismic waves is a(an) _____.

6. Which way of measuring earthquake strength is based on the kind of information shown in the drawing?

_____

Earthquakes

Locating the Epicenter (pages 56–57)

Key Concept: Geologists use seismic waves to locate an earthquake's epicenter.

- The epicenter is the point on the surface that lies directly above an earthquake's focus. Scientists use P waves and S waves to find an earthquake's epicenter.

- P waves travel faster than S waves. So P waves arrive at a seismograph sooner than S waves. The longer it takes S waves to reach the seismograph after P waves have arrived, the farther away the epicenter is.

- To find the exact location of the epicenter, you need seismographs in three different places. You can draw a circle around each seismograph to show how far the epicenter is from that seismograph. The point where all three circles cross is the epicenter.

Answer the following questions. Use your textbook and the ideas above.

7. Suppose it takes a long time for S waves to reach a seismograph after P waves have arrived. What does that tell you about the earthquake? Circle the letter of the correct answer.

   a. The earthquake was strong.

   b. The earthquake was close to the surface.

   c. The earthquake was far away.

8. Is the following sentence true or false? One seismograph can tell you exactly where the epicenter

   of an earthquake is. _____

Earthquakes

9. The map shows three different seismographs in the United States. Each circle shows the distance from a seismograph to the epicenter of an earthquake. Where is the epicenter? Circle the letter of the correct answer.

　a. A

　b. B

　c. C

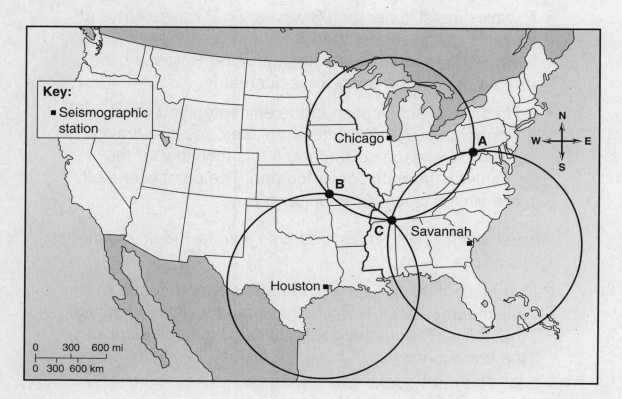

Monitoring Earthquakes (pages 60–65)

The Seismograph (page 61)

Key Concept: **Seismic waves cause the seismograph's drum to vibrate. But the suspended weight with the pen attached moves very little. Therefore, the pen stays in place and records the drum's vibrations.**

- In a simple seismograph, a pen hangs down from a heavy weight. The point of the pen touches graph paper that is wrapped around a cylinder, or drum. As the drum turns, the pen draws a line on the paper.

- When an earthquake shakes the ground, the pen hardly moves because of the weight. But the drum shakes with the ground. The shaking of the drum makes the line on the paper jagged. The more jagged the line is, the stronger or closer the earthquake was.

Answer the following question. Use your textbook and the ideas above.

1. The seismograph readings are for two different earthquakes. Circle the letter of the seismograph reading that shows an earthquake that was stronger or closer.

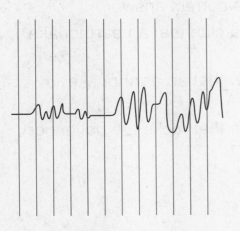

a.

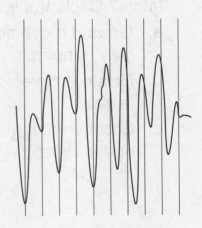

b.

Earthquakes

Instruments That Monitor Faults (pages 62–63)

Key Concept: **To monitor faults, geologists have developed instruments to measure changes in elevation, tilting of the land surface, and ground movements along faults.**

- Ground movements near a fault are a clue that an earthquake might happen. So scientists measure ground movements near faults. They use tiltmeters, creep meters, and GPS satellites.

- Tiltmeters show how much the ground is tilting, or tipping. A tiltmeter works like a carpenter's level. When the ground tilts, water inside a glass bulb shows how much tilting there is.

- Creep meters show how far the sides of a fault have moved in opposite directions. A creep meter uses a wire stretched across the fault. The wire gets longer when the two sides move apart.

- Scientists put markers along both sides of a fault. GPS satellites detect tiny movements of the markers in any direction.

Answer the following questions. Use your textbook and the ideas above.

2. Why do scientists measure ground movements near faults? Circle the letter of the correct answer.

   a. Ground movements are a clue that an earthquake may happen.

   b. Ground movements show that an earthquake is over.

   c. Ground movements show that rocks are no longer under stress.

Earthquakes

3. Fill in the blanks in the concept map about instruments that measure ground movements.

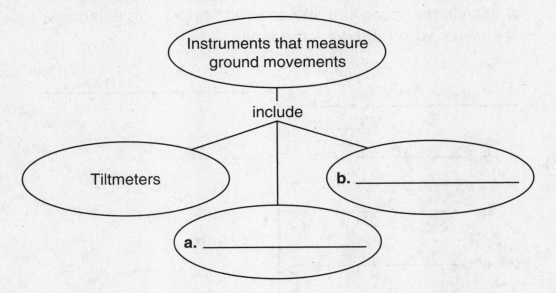

Using Seismographic Data (pages 64–65)

Key Concept: **Seismographs and fault-monitoring devices provide data used to map faults and detect changes along faults. Geologists are also trying to use these data to develop a method of predicting earthquakes.**

- When seismic waves reach a fault, they bounce off it, like a ball bouncing off a wall. Seismographs record the waves that bounce back. Scientists can use the seismographic data to find the fault.

- Seismographic data can also be used to learn how easily rocks move at a fault. At faults where rocks do not move easily, stress builds up, and big earthquakes are likely.

- Even with data from many sources, scientists cannot predict exactly where or when an earthquake will happen.

Name _____ Date _____ Class _____

Earthquakes

*Answer the following questions. Use your textbook and the
ideas on page 37.*

4. Circle the letter that shows what happens to seismic
waves when they reach a fault.

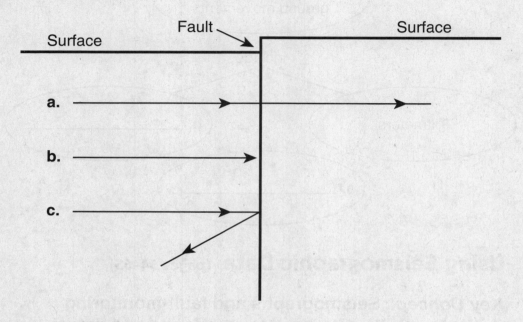

5. Circle the letter of the choice that describes where big
earthquakes are likely to happen.
   a. at faults where rocks move easily
   b. at faults where rocks do not move easily
   c. at rocks where there are no faults

6. Is the following sentence true or false? Scientists can
now predict exactly where and when earthquakes will

   happen. _____

Earthquake Safety (pages 68–73)

Earthquake Risk (page 69)

Key Concept: **Geologists can determine earthquake risk by locating where faults are active and where past earthquakes have occurred.**

- Earthquakes are most likely at faults along the boundary between two plates.

- The Pacific plate and the North American plate meet along the Pacific coast of the United States. The coasts of California, Washington, and Alaska all have a high risk of earthquakes.

- The eastern United States is far from plate boundaries. Only a few big earthquakes have happened in the eastern United States in the past. So this part of the country has a low risk of earthquakes.

Answer the following questions. Use your textbook and the ideas above.

1. Is the following sentence true or false? Earthquakes are most likely to happen far from plate boundaries.

   _____

2. Circle the letter of each sentence that is true about earthquake risk in the United States.

   a. The risk of earthquakes is high along the Pacific coast.

   b. There is no risk of earthquakes in the East.

   c. Alaska has a high risk of earthquakes.

Earthquakes

How Earthquakes Cause Damage
(pages 70–71)

Key Concept: **Causes of earthquake damage include shaking, liquefaction, aftershocks, and tsunamis.**

- When an earthquake happens, seismic waves cause the ground to shake. The shaking can destroy buildings and break gas and water pipes.

- Sometimes the shaking turns soft soil into mud. This is called **liquefaction** (lik wih FAK shun). Liquefaction can make buildings sink.

- Smaller earthquakes, called **aftershocks**, can follow a big earthquake. Aftershocks add to the damage done by the big earthquake.

- An earthquake on the ocean floor can cause a huge ocean wave, called a **tsunami** (tsoo NAH mee). Tsunamis can cause a great deal of damage along coasts.

Answer the following question. Use your textbook and the ideas above.

3. Read the words in the box. In each sentence below, fill in one of the words.

aftershock	tsunami	liquefaction	shaking

   a. When an earthquake causes soft soil to turn to mud, it is called _____.

   b. A smaller earthquake that follows a big earthquake is called a(an) _____.

   c. A huge ocean wave caused by an earthquake is a(an) _____.

Earthquakes

Steps to Earthquake Safety (page 71)

Key Concept: **The best way to protect yourself in an earthquake is to drop, cover, and hold.**

- If you are indoors when an earthquake hits, you should drop down under a sturdy table or desk. Then, you should cover your head and neck with your arms and hold onto the table or desk.

- If you are outdoors when an earthquake hits, you should move to an open area such as a playground. You should sit on the ground so you will not be thrown to the ground when the earthquake shakes.

- After an earthquake, you may have no electricity or running water for a while. Stores and roads may also be closed.

- If you live where earthquakes are likely, you should have an earthquake kit. The kit should contain canned food, water, and other emergency supplies.

Answer the following questions. Use your textbook and the ideas above.

4. Is the following sentence true or false? The best place to be if you are indoors when an earthquake hits is under a sturdy table or desk. _____

5. Circle the letter of the safest place to be if you are outdoors when an earthquake hits.
   a. beside a tall building
   b. under a bridge
   c. in the middle of an open field

Earthquakes

Designing Safer Buildings (pages 72–73)

Key Concept: To reduce earthquake damage, new buildings must be made stronger and more flexible. Older buildings may be modified to withstand stronger quakes.

- The main danger in earthquakes is falling buildings and objects. To reduce this danger, plywood can be added to walls to make buildings stronger. Tall furniture can also be attached to walls.

- Another danger in earthquakes is liquefaction. To reduce this danger, buildings can be attached to solid rock below the soil. This keeps the buildings from sinking if the soil turns to mud.

- When gas and water pipes break, it may cause fires and flooding. To reduce this danger, pipes can be changed so they bend instead of break when the ground shakes.

Answer the following questions. Use your textbook and the ideas above.

6. Is the following sentence true or false? The main danger in earthquakes is falling buildings and objects.

_____

7. Circle the letter of a way to reduce earthquake damage.

    a. add plywood to the walls of buildings

    b. change pipes so they do not bend

    c. attach buildings to soil instead of rock

Volcanoes and Plate Tectonics (pages 82–85)

Volcanoes and Plate Boundaries
(pages 83–84)

Key Concept: Volcanic belts form along the boundaries of Earth's plates.

- A **volcano** is a weak spot in the crust where melted material comes to the surface. The melted material is called **magma.** Magma rises to the surface because it is less dense than solid rock.

- Most volcanoes happen at plate boundaries. Remember, plate boundaries are where two plates pull apart or push together.

- Where plates pull apart, magma rises and pours out of cracks in the crust.

- Where plates push together, the denser plate sinks into the mantle. Some of the sinking plate melts and forms magma. The magma rises and pours out of cracks.

- Once magma reaches the surface, it is called **lava.** As lava cools, it forms solid rock.

- Lava can build up to form mountains. When the mountains are on the ocean floor, islands form if the mountains poke above the water's surface.

Answer the following questions. Use your textbook and the ideas above.

1. A weak spot in the crust where melted material comes to the surface is a(an) _____.

Volcanoes

2. Read the words in the box. In each sentence below, fill in one of the words.

> rock   lava   magma   mantle

    a. Melted material beneath the surface inside a

    volcano is called _____.

    b. Once melted material reaches the surface, it is

    called _____.

    c. When lava cools to a solid, it forms

    _____.

3. The diagram shows how some volcanoes form. During subduction, Plate _____ sinks beneath Plate _____ and melts, forming magma.

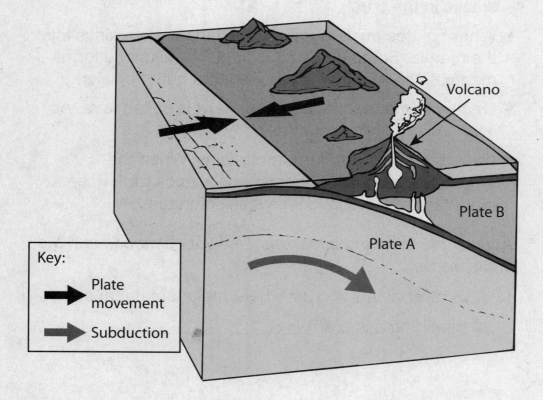

Volcano

Plate B

Plate A

Key:

→ Plate movement

→ Subduction

Name _____ Date _____ Class _____

Volcanoes

Hot Spot Volcanoes (page 85)

Key Concept: **A volcano forms above a hot spot when magma erupts through the crust and reaches the surface.**

- A **hot spot** is a place where material rises from deep in the mantle. The material forms magma.

- If the magma breaks through the crust, a volcano forms. Hot spot volcanoes on the ocean floor can become islands. This how the Hawaiian Islands formed.

- Some hot spots are under the middle of plates, far from plate boundaries. For example, there is a hot spot under the North American plate at Yellowstone National Park in Wyoming.

Answer the following questions. Use your textbook and the ideas above.

4. Circle the letter of each sentence that is true about hot spots.
   a. Hot spots occur only at plate boundaries.
   b. Hot spots can cause volcanoes.
   c. Hot spots can cause islands to form.

5. Is the following sentence true or false? The Hawaiian Islands were formed by hot spot volcanoes.

   _____

Volcanoes

Properties of Magma (pages 87–90)

Physical and Chemical Properties
(pages 87–88)

Key Concept: Each substance has a particular set of physical and chemical properties. These properties can be used to identify a substance or to predict how it will behave.

- Like other substances, magma has a certain set of properties, or traits. Properties can be physical or chemical.

- **Physical properties** are traits that can be observed without changing what a substance is made of. Examples of physical properties are hardness and color.

- **Chemical properties** are traits that can be observed only by changing what a substance is made of. An example of a chemical property is being able to burn. Another example is being able to combine with other substances.

Answer the following questions. Use your textbook and the ideas above.

1. Circle the letter of an example of a physical property.
   a. being able to burn
   b. being able to combine with other substances
   c. hardness

2. Is the following sentence true or false? You can observe a chemical property without changing what a substance is made of. _____

Volcanoes

3. Fill in the blanks in the concept map about properties of substances.

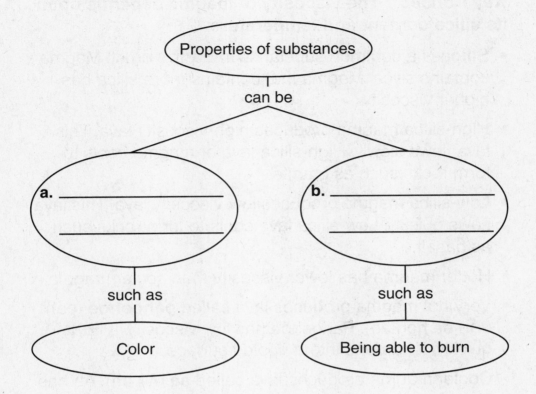

What Is Viscosity? (page 88)

Key Concept: **Because liquids differ in viscosity, some liquids flow more easily than others.**

- **Viscosity** (vis KAHS uh tee) is a physical property of liquids. How well a liquid flows depends on its viscosity.

- A liquid with high viscosity is thick. It flows slowly. An example of a liquid with high viscosity is honey.

- A liquid with low viscosity is thin. It flows quickly. An example of a liquid with low viscosity is water.

Answer the following question. Use your textbook and the ideas above.

4. Is the following sentence true or false? Honey has

   higher viscosity than water. _____

Viscosity of Magma (pages 89–90)

Key Concept: The viscosity of magma depends upon its silica content and temperature.

- **Silica** is a common substance in Earth's crust. Magma contains silica. Magma that contains more silica has higher viscosity.

- High-silica magma produces high-viscosity lava. This lava flows slowly. High-silica lava or magma cools to form rocks such as granite.

- Low-silica magma produces low-viscosity lava. This lava flows quickly. Low-silica lava cools to form rocks such as basalt.

- Hotter magma has lower viscosity than cooler magma.

- Very hot magma produces lava called **pahoehoe** (pah HOH ee hoh ee). Pahoehoe has low viscosity. It flows quickly. It hardens into a rippled surface.

- Cooler magma produces lava called **aa** (AH ah). Aa has high viscosity. It flows slowly. It hardens into rough chunks.

Answer the following questions. Use your textbook and the ideas above.

5. Is the following sentence true or false? High-silica magma has high viscosity. _____

6. Fill in the blanks in the table about kinds of lava.

Kinds of Lava		
Kind of Lava	**Temperature**	**Viscosity**
Pahoehoe	hotter	**a.** _____
b. _____	cooler	higher

Volcanic Eruptions (pages 91–98)

Magma Reaches Earth's Surface
(pages 92–93)

Key Concept: **When a volcano erupts, the force of the expanding gases pushes magma from the magma chamber through the pipe until it flows or explodes out of the vent.**

- A volcano has a pocket of magma below the surface, called a **magma chamber**. A long tube, called a **pipe**, connects the magma chamber to the surface.

- At the top of a pipe is an opening called a **vent**. Magma leaves the volcano through the vent and becomes lava. The area covered by lava as it pours out of a vent is called a **lava flow**.

- As magma nears the surface, pressure on the magma falls. Dissolved gases in magma start to form bubbles. The bubbles take up more space than the dissolved gases. The bubbles force magma out of the vent, like the bubbles that force warm pop out of a bottle.

Answer the following questions. Use your textbook and the ideas above.

1. Read the words in the box. In each sentence below, fill in one of the words.

pipe	vent	chamber

   a. Magma leaves a volcano through a

   _____.

   b. Magma flows from a magma chamber to the

   surface through a _____.

2. Circle the letter of the choice that explains why a volcano erupts.

   a. Dissolved gases in magma form bubbles, forcing the magma out of a vent.

   b. Magma gets warmer and less dense as it nears the surface, causing the magma to flow out of a pipe.

   c. Pressure on magma increases as it nears the surface, forcing the magma into a magma chamber.

3. Read the words in the box. Use the words to fill in the blanks in the diagram of a volcano.

| Magma chamber | Pipe | Lava flow | Vent |

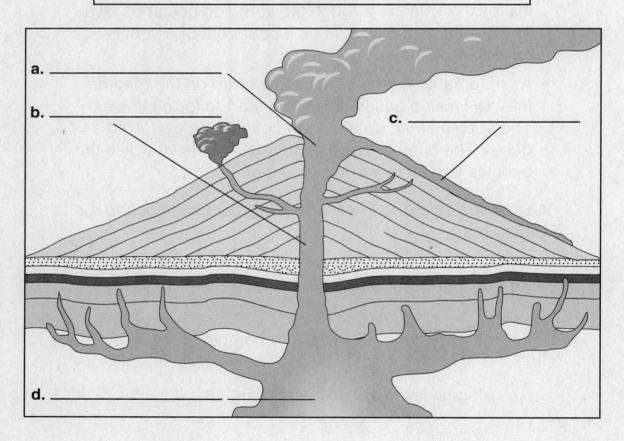

a. _____

b. _____

c. _____

d. _____

Volcanoes

Kinds of Volcanic Eruptions (pages 94–96)

Key Concept: Geologists classify volcanic eruptions as quiet or explosive.

- When magma pours out of a volcano, it is called a volcanic eruption. An eruption can happen slowly and quietly. Or an eruption can happen all at once with an explosion. How a volcano erupts depends on the magma.

- A volcano erupts quietly if the magma is low in silica and flows easily. The lava may flow for many kilometers before it starts to harden into rock.

- A volcano erupts with an explosion if the magma is high in silica and does not flow easily. Magma builds up in the pipe until it explodes out of the vent. The lava cools quickly. The hard lava pieces range in size from ashes and cinders to very large chunks called bombs.

- Both kinds of eruptions can do damage. A quiet eruption can cover a large area with a layer of lava. An explosive eruption can start fires and bury towns in ash.

Answer the following questions. Use your textbook and the ideas above.

4. What explains whether a volcano has a quiet or explosive eruption? Circle the letter of the correct answer.
    a. how much space there is in the magma chamber
    b. how much magma there is in the pipe
    c. how much silica there is in the magma

5. Is the following sentence true or false? Only explosive eruptions do damage. _____

6. Label each circle in the Venn diagram with the kind of eruption it describes.

a. _____   b. _____

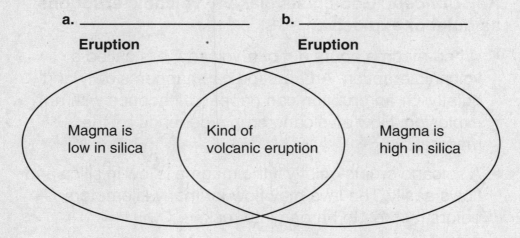

Stages of Volcanic Activity (pages 97–98)

Key Concept: Geologists often use the terms *active, dormant,* or *extinct* to describe a volcano's stage of activity.

- A volcano is active when it is erupting or showing signs that it will erupt soon.

- A volcano is **dormant** when it is no longer erupting but is likely to erupt again in the future. A dormant volcano may not erupt for thousands of years. But it can become active at any time.

- A volcano is **extinct** when it is no longer likely to erupt, even in the future.

- Scientists try to predict when a volcano will erupt. They watch for signs that magma is moving upward. Scientists often can predict when a volcano will erupt. But they cannot predict what kind of eruption or how strong an eruption it will be.

Volcanoes

Answer the following questions. Use your textbook and the ideas on page 52.

7. Read the words in the box. In each sentence below, fill in one of the words.

> extinct   active   dormant

  a. A volcano that is no longer likely to erupt, even in the future, is _____.

  b. A volcano that is no longer erupting but is likely to erupt again in the future is _____.

8. How do scientists try to predict volcanoes? Circle the letter of the correct answer.

  a. by measuring the amount of silica in magma

  b. by measuring the size of the magma chamber

  c. by watching for signs that magma is moving upward

9. Is the following sentence true or false? Scientists sometimes can predict when a volcano is about to erupt. _____

Volcanoes

Volcanic Landforms (pages 99–105)

Landforms From Lava and Ash
(pages 100–102)

Key Concept: Volcanic eruptions create landforms made of lava, ash, and other materials. These landforms include shield volcanoes, cinder cone volcanoes, composite volcanoes, and lava plateaus.

- A **shield volcano** is a gently sloping mountain. It forms when a volcano erupts quietly. Thin layers of lava build up slowly over a large area around the vent.

- A **cinder cone** is a steep, cone-shaped hill or small mountain. It forms when a volcano erupts explosively. Ashes, cinders, and bombs pile up around the vent.

- A **composite volcano** is a tall, cone-shaped mountain. It forms when a volcano erupts quietly and then explosively, over and over again. Layers of lava are followed by layers of ash, cinders, and bombs.

- Sometimes lava forms a plateau instead of a mountain. A lava plateau is a high, level area. It forms when thin lava flows out of many long cracks.

- If a magma chamber empties, a volcano can collapse. This leaves a huge hole called a **caldera** (kal DAIR uh). A caldera may fill with water and form a lake.

Answer the following questions. Use your textbook and the ideas above.

1. If a volcano collapses, it leaves a huge hole called a(an) _____.

2. Fill in the blank beside each drawing with the kind of volcano the drawing shows.

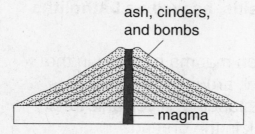

a. _____

_____

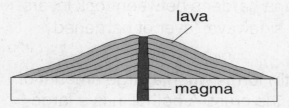

b. _____

_____

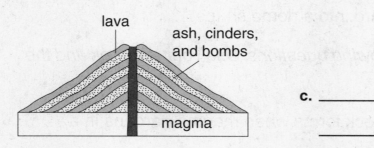

c. _____

_____

3. Circle the letter of the choice that describes how a lava plateau forms.

   a. Thick lava erupts from a central vent.

   b. Thin lava flows out of many long cracks.

   c. Thick lava erupts from a caldera.

Volcanoes

Landforms From Magma (pages 103–104)

Key Concept: **Features formed by magma include volcanic necks, dikes, and sills, as well as batholiths and dome mountains.**

- A **volcanic neck** forms when magma hardens in the pipe of a volcano. Softer rock around the pipe wears away, leaving just the neck standing. A volcanic neck looks like a giant tooth stuck in the ground.

- A **dike** forms when magma hardens across rock layers. A dike is a vertical, or up-and-down, layer of hardened magma.

- A **sill** forms when magma hardens between rock layers. A sill is a horizontal, or sideways, layer of hardened magma.

- A **batholith** (BATH uh lith) forms when a large amount of magma hardens inside the crust. A batholith is a large rock mass. It may become part of a mountain range.

- A dome mountain forms when a batholith or smaller chunk of hardened magma is pushed up to the surface. The hardened magma forces the layers of rock above it to bend upward into a dome shape.

Answer the following questions. Use your textbook and the ideas above.

4. A volcanic neck forms when magma hardens in a volcano's _____.

5. Circle the letter of each sentence that is true about batholiths.
   a. Batholiths form on the surface.
   b. Batholiths are large masses of rock.
   c. Batholiths may form dome mountains.

6. Fill in the blanks to label the dike and the sill.

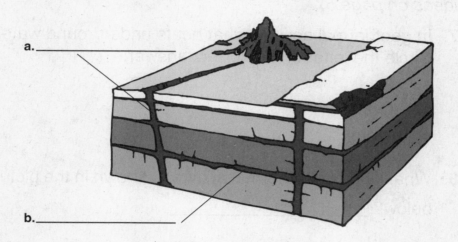

a. _____

b. _____

Geothermal Activity (pages 104–105)

Key Concept: **Hot springs and geysers are types of geothermal activity that are often found in areas of present or past volcanic activity.**

- Magma below the surface can heat underground water. The heating of underground water by magma is called **geothermal activity**. Geothermal activity is common where there are volcanoes.

- A hot spring forms when water heated by magma rises to the surface and collects in a natural pool.

- A **geyser** (GY zur) forms when hot water and steam are trapped underground in a narrow crack. Pressure builds up until the hot water and steam erupt from the ground. This happens over and over again. Old Faithful is a geyser in Yellowstone National Park. It erupts about once an hour.

- Hot water from underground can be piped into homes to heat them. This is how many people in Iceland heat their homes.

- Steam from underground can be piped into electric power plants. In the power plants, the heat energy in the steam is turned into electric energy.

Volcanoes

Answer the following questions. Use your textbook and the ideas on page 57.

7. In geothermal activity, what heats underground water? Circle the letter of the correct answer.

    a. lava

    b. steam

    c. magma

8. What kind of geothermal activity is shown in the picture below? _____

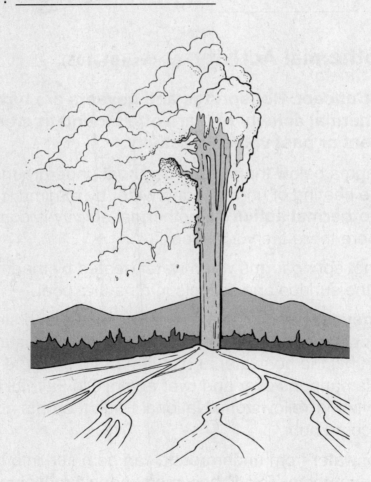

9. Is the following sentence true or false? Underground water and steam can be used for energy. _____

Properties of Minerals
(pages 114–122)

What Is a Mineral? (pages 114–115)

Key Concept: **A mineral is a naturally occurring, inorganic solid that has a crystal structure and a definite chemical composition.**

- A **mineral** has all five of the following characteristics.

- A mineral must be formed by natural processes. For example, a mineral might be formed by the cooling of magma.

- A mineral must be **inorganic**. Something that is inorganic was never part of a living thing.

- A mineral is always a solid. A mineral is not a liquid or a gas.

- The particles that make up a mineral always line up in a certain pattern that keeps repeating. The repeating pattern forms a solid called a **crystal**. A crystal has flat sides that meet at sharp edges.

- A mineral has a certain "recipe." For example, the mineral quartz is always made of oxygen and silicon, and there is always twice as much oxygen as silicon.

Answer the following questions. Use your textbook and the ideas above.

1. Circle the letter of each sentence that is true about minerals.
   a. Some minerals are gases.
   b. Some minerals come from living things.
   c. All minerals have a definite makeup.

Name _____ Date _____ Class _____

Minerals

2. Read the words in the box. In each sentence below, fill in one of the words.

crystal	inorganic	solid	mineral	silicon

  a. Something that was never part of a living thing is

     _____.

  b. A solid made up of particles in a repeating pattern

     is a(an) _____.

  c. A material that is not a liquid or a gas is a(an)

     _____.

  d. Quartz is an example of a(an)

     _____.

3. Fill in the blanks in the concept map about minerals.

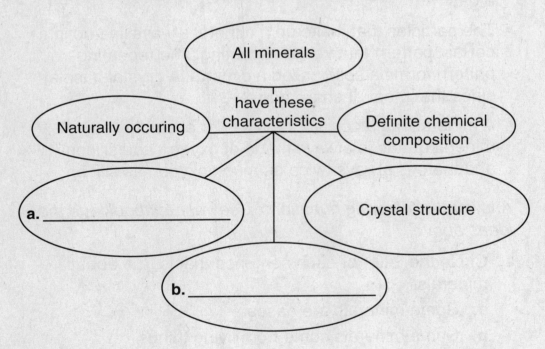

Identifying Minerals (pages 116–122)

Key Concept: **Each mineral has characteristic properties that can be used to identify it.**

- There are almost 4,000 known minerals. You can tell minerals apart by their properties. You can observe some properties just by looking at minerals. You can observe other properties only by testing minerals.

- Color is a property that is easy to observe. Only a few minerals can be identified by color alone. Malachite is one of them. Malachite is always green, and no other mineral is exactly the same color.

- The **streak** of a mineral is the color of its powder. You can see streak by rubbing a mineral against rough tile. The streak color may not be the same as the color of the mineral itself.

- **Luster** depends on how a mineral reflects light. A mineral's luster is described by a word such as *shiny, metallic, waxy, dull,* or *greasy.*

- A mineral's density is always the same. Remember, density is the amount of mass in a given volume of a substance. Density equals mass divided by volume.

- Each mineral has a certain hardness. Hardness is measured by scratching a mineral. A mineral can be scratched by any mineral harder than itself. The softest mineral is talc. The hardest mineral is diamond.

- A mineral's crystals always have the same shape. For example, a mineral's crystals might be shaped like cubes.

- Some minerals split easily into flat pieces. These minerals have a property called **cleavage**. Mica is a mineral with cleavage.

- Other minerals do not split easily into flat pieces. These minerals have a property called **fracture**. A mineral with fracture always breaks into pieces with a certain shape. For example, quartz always breaks into pieces shaped like seashells.

- Some minerals can be identified by special properties. For example, magnetite is magnetic. It attracts iron.

Answer the following questions. Use your textbook and the ideas on page 61 and above.

4. Read the words in the box. In each sentence below, fill in one of the words.

streak	luster	density
hardness	cleavage	fracture

a. If a mineral does not split easily into flat pieces, it has a property called _____.

b. The color of a mineral's powder is its _____.

c. How a mineral reflects light is its _____.

d. If a mineral splits easily into flat pieces, it has a property called _____.

e. The amount of mass in a given volume of a substance is the substance's _____.

f. A property measured by scratching a mineral is _____.

5. Fill in the blanks to label the mineral that has cleavage and the mineral that has fracture.

a. _____   **b.** _____

6. The table shows scratch-test results for five minerals. Circle the letter of the choice that shows the minerals in the correct order, from softest to hardest.

  a. feldspar, talc, quartz, calcite, diamond

  b. talc, calcite, feldspar, quartz, diamond

  c. talc, quartz, feldspar, diamond, calcite

Scratch-Test Results for Five Minerals				
Talc	**Diamond**	**Calcite**	**Quartz**	**Feldspar**
scratched by all	scratched by none	scratched by feldspar, quartz, diamond	scratched by diamond	scratched by quartz, diamond

Minerals

How Minerals Form (pages 124–127)

Minerals From Magma and Lava (page 125)

Key Concept: **Minerals form as hot magma cools inside the crust, or as lava hardens on the surface. When these liquids cool to a solid state, they form crystals.**

- Minerals form in a process called crystallization. In **crystallization**, particles of a substance form crystals. Remember, crystals are solids that have their particles lined up in repeating patterns. Crystals have flat sides and sharp edges.

- Many minerals form when magma and lava cool. The size of the crystals that form depends on how fast the magma or lava cools. When it cools slowly, there is more time for large crystals to form.

- When magma cools deep under Earth's surface, it cools very slowly. The crystals that form are very large.

- When magma cools closer to the surface, it cools faster. The crystals that form are smaller.

- When magma erupts to the surface and forms lava, it cools even faster. The crystals that form from lava are very small.

Answer the following questions. Use your textbook and the ideas above.

1. Is the following sentence true or false? Very few minerals form from magma or lava. _____

2. Is the following sentence true or false? A mineral that forms when magma cools deep inside Earth has very small crystals. _____

3. Circle the letter of the process in which particles of a substance line up in a repeating pattern.

    a. mineralization

    b. eruption

    c. crystallization

Minerals From Solutions (pages 125–127)

Key Concept: **When elements and compounds that are dissolved in water leave a solution, crystallization occurs.**

- Substances that form minerals may be dissolved in water. The water and dissolved substances form a solution. A **solution** is a mixture in which one substance is dissolved in another.

- Some dissolved substances form mineral crystals when they leave a solution. Dissolved substances can leave a solution in two ways.

- Dissolved substances can leave a solution when the solution evaporates, or turns into gases. This happens on Earth's surface. For example, the mineral halite formed when ancient seas evaporated.

- Dissolved substances can leave a solution when the solution cools. This happens below Earth's surface. Underground water heated by magma dissolves many substances. When the water cools, minerals come out of the solution and form crystals.

- A **vein** is a narrow band of minerals that lies between rock layers. Veins look like streaks of fudge in vanilla fudge ice cream. Veins form when solutions of hot water flow through cracks and then cool. Silver is a mineral that may form in veins.

Answer the following questions. Use your textbook and the ideas on page 65.

4. Read the words in the box. In each sentence below, fill in one of the words.

solution	silver	halite	vein

   a. A narrow band of a mineral that lies between rock layers is a _____.

   b. A mixture in which one substance is dissolved in another is a _____.

   c. A mineral that formed when ancient seas evaporated is _____.

5. Fill in the blanks in the concept map about how minerals form from solutions.

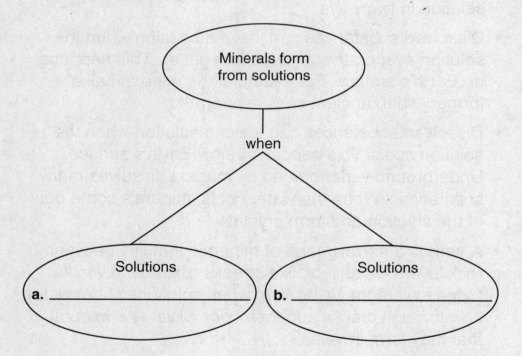

Using Mineral Resources

(pages 130–135)

The Uses of Minerals (page 131)

Key Concept: **Minerals are the source of gemstones, metals, and a variety of materials used to make many products.**

- A **gemstone** is a hard, colorful mineral that is shiny. Gemstones are used mainly for jewelry. Examples are rubies, sapphires, and diamonds.

- Minerals such as copper, gold, and silver are called metals. Metals are usually softer than gemstones. Metals are used for wires, jewelry, tools, and buildings.

- Other useful minerals include quartz and gypsum. Quartz is used to make glass. Gypsum is used to make cement.

Answer the following questions. Use your textbook and the ideas above.

1. A hard, colorful mineral that is shiny is a(an)

   _____.

2. Circle the letter of a mineral that is might be used to make wire.
   a. gypsum
   b. ruby
   c. copper

3. Circle the letter of a mineral that is used to make glass.
   a. quartz
   b. sapphire
   c. silver

Minerals

Producing Metals From Minerals

(pages 132–135)

Key Concept: **To produce metal from a mineral, a rock containing the mineral must be located through prospecting and mined, or removed from the ground. Then the rock must be processed to extract the metal.**

- Most metals are found in rocks that also contain other substances. An **ore** is a rock that contains a metal or other useful mineral.

- A prospector is someone who looks for ore. To find ore, a prospector might look at rocks on the surface and study maps of underground rocks.

- Mining is removing ore from the ground. There are different kinds of mines. For example, in a shaft mine, miners dig tunnels to follow veins of ore.

- **Smelting** is removing metal from ore. For example, the ore hematite is smelted to remove iron. In smelting, hematite is crushed, mixed with other materials, and heated.

- After smelting, a metal may be mixed with other substances to make an alloy. An **alloy** is a solid mixture containing at least one metal. For example, iron is mixed with carbon to form the alloy steel. Steel is harder and stronger than pure iron.

Answer the following questions. Use your textbook and the ideas above.

4. Is the following sentence true or false? Most metals are found in the ground in pure form. _____

Minerals

5. Read the words in the box. In each sentence below, fill in one of the words.

ore	miner	smelting
alloy	hematite	prospector

a. A solid mixture containing at least one metal is

a(an) _____.

b. A rock containing a metal or other useful mineral is

a(an) _____.

c. The process of removing metal from ore is called

_____.

d. Someone who looks for ore is a(an)

_____.

e. Iron occurs in an ore called

_____.

6. Fill in the blank in the flowchart about producing metals.

Steps in Producing Metals

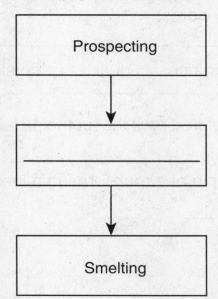

Classifying Rocks (pages 144–147)

Mineral Composition and Color (page 145)

Key Concept: **When studying a rock sample, geologists observe the rock's mineral composition and color.**

- Rocks are mixtures of minerals and other materials. A rock may contain one or more minerals. **Granite** contains at least four minerals: feldspar, quartz, hornblende, and mica.

- About 20 minerals make up most of the rocks in Earth's crust. These 20 minerals are known as **rock-forming minerals**.

- A rock's color may help identify its minerals. For example, granite is usually light-colored because it is made of minerals that contain a lot of silica.

- To identify the minerals in most rocks, you also need to see the shape and color of the mineral crystals.

Answer the following questions. Use your textbook and the ideas above.

1. Read the words in the box. In each sentence below, fill in one of the words.

granite   quartz   crystal

    a. A light-colored rock that contains feldspar and other minerals is _____.

    b. An example of a rock-forming mineral is

    _____.

2. Is the following sentence true or false? The color of a rock lets you identify all the minerals that the rock contains. _____

Texture (page 146)

Key Concept: **When studying a rock sample, geologists also observe the rock's texture.**

- Most rocks are made up of particles, called **grains**. Grains are particles of minerals or other rocks.

- Grains give rocks their texture. A rock's **texture** is how the rock's surface looks and feels. For example, a rock's texture could be smooth or rough. Texture is used to help identify rocks.

- The grains in rock may be big or small. Some grains are big enough to see easily. Other grains are too small to see, even with a microscope. Rocks with big grains have a rougher texture than rocks with small grains.

- The grains in rock have many different shapes. For example, some grains are smooth and rounded. Other grains are jagged.

- The grains in rock often form patterns. Some rocks have grains in flat layers like a stack of pancakes. Other rocks have grains in bands of different colors.

Answer the following questions. Use your textbook and the ideas above.

3. Draw a line from each term to its meaning.

Term	Meaning
grains	**a.** how a rock's surface looks and feels
texture	**b.** the particles that make up rocks

Rocks

4. Read the words in the box. In each sentence below, fill in one of the words.

| grains | bands | texture |

a. Rocks are made up of particles called

_____.

b. If you say the surface of a rock feels smooth, you

are describing the rock's _____.

5. Fill in the blanks in the concept map about grains in rock.

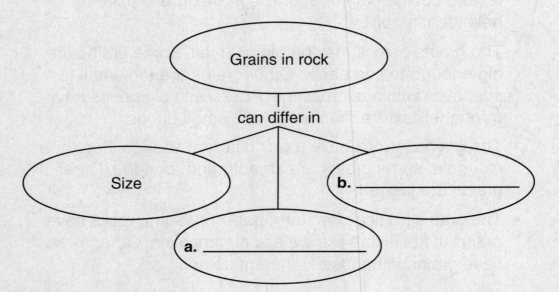

6. Circle the letter of each choice that describes a grain pattern in rock.

a. Grains are stacked in flat layers.

b. Grains are large with jagged edges.

c. Grains are in bands of different colors.

How Rocks Form (page 147)

Key Concept: **Geologists classify rocks into three major groups: igneous rock, sedimentary rock, and metamorphic rock.**

- Rocks are classified into the three major groups based on how they form.

- **Igneous** (IG nee us) **rock** forms when magma or lava cools. Igneous rock forms near volcanoes.

- **Sedimentary** (sed uh MEN tur ee) **rock** forms when particles are pressed and stuck together. Sedimentary rock slowly builds up in layers. Newer layers cover up older layers.

- **Metamorphic** (met uh MAWR fik) **rock** forms when heat and pressure change any kind of rock. Metamorphic rock forms below Earth's surface.

Answer the following question. Use your textbook and the ideas above.

7. Label each diagram with the kind of rock that could form.

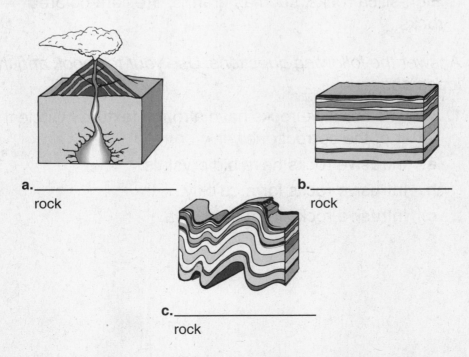

a._____
rock

b._____
rock

c._____
rock

Igneous Rocks (pages 148–151)

Classifying Igneous Rocks (pages 148–150)

Key Concept: Igneous rocks are classified according to their origin, texture, and mineral composition.

- Igneous rock is rock that forms from magma or lava. Igneous rock may form on or below Earth's surface. Where igneous rock forms is its origin.

- **Extrusive rock** is igneous rock that forms on Earth's surface, when lava cools. Lava cools quickly, forming small crystals. As a result, extrusive rock has a smooth texture. The most common extrusive rock is basalt.

- **Intrusive rock** is igneous rock that forms below Earth's surface, when magma cools. Magma cools slowly, forming big crystals. As a result, intrusive rock has a rough texture. The most common intrusive rock is granite.

- Igneous rocks differ in how much silica they contain. Low-silica rocks, such as basalt, are dark-colored rocks. High-silica rocks, such as granite, are light-colored rocks.

Answer the following questions. Use your textbook and the ideas above.

1. Why do intrusive rocks have a rough texture? Circle the letter of the correct answer.

    a. Intrusive rocks have big crystals.

    b. Intrusive rocks form quickly.

    c. Intrusive rocks form from lava.

Name _____ Date _____ Class _____

Rocks

2. Label each circle in the Venn diagram with the kind of igneous rock it describes.

a. _____   b. _____
   Rock   **Rock**

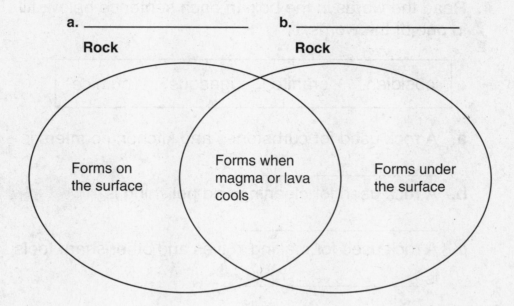

Forms on the surface

Forms when magma or lava cools

Forms under the surface

3. If an igneous rock is light-colored it probably contains a lot of _____.

Uses of Igneous Rocks (page 151)

Key Concept: **People throughout history have used igneous rock for tools and building materials.**

- Igneous rocks have several uses. Examples of useful igneous rocks are granite, pumice, and obsidian.

- Granite is very hard and dense. Granite has long been used for buildings and bridges. Today, granite is also used for curbstones and kitchen counters.

- Pumice is very rough. Pumice is used for cleaning and polishing.

- Obsidian is sharp and smooth like glass. Obsidian was used by ancient native Americans to make knives and other sharp tools.

Name _____ Date _____ Class _____

Rocks

Answer the following question. Use your textbook and the ideas on page 75.

4. Read the words in the box. In each sentence below, fill in one of the words.

obsidian	granite	igneous	pumice

a. A rock used for curbstones and kitchen counters is

_____.

b. A rock used for cleaning and polishing is

_____.

c. A rock used for making knives and other sharp tools

is _____.

Sedimentary Rocks

(pages 152–156)

From Sediment to Rock (pages 152–153)

Key Concept: **Most sedimentary rocks are formed through a series of processes: erosion, deposition, compaction, and cementation.**

- **Sediment** is the particles that make up sedimentary rock. Sediment may include pieces of rock, shell, or bone.

- Most sediment comes from erosion. In **erosion**, moving water, wind, or ice loosens and carries away pieces of rock.

- When the moving water, wind, or ice slows down, it drops the sediment. This is called **deposition**.

- Layers of sediment build up over millions of years. Newer layers press down on older layers. This squeezes the sediment together. The squeezing is called **compaction**.

- Water seeps between sediment particles. Dissolved minerals in the water form crystals. The crystals "glue" the sediment particles together. This is called **cementation**.

Answer the following questions. Use your textbook and the ideas above.

1. Circle the letter of the process that loosens and carries away pieces of rock.
   - **a.** compaction
   - **b.** erosion
   - **c.** deposition

2. Fill in the blanks in the flowchart showing the series of processes that forms sedimentary rocks.

Process That Form Sedimentary Rocks

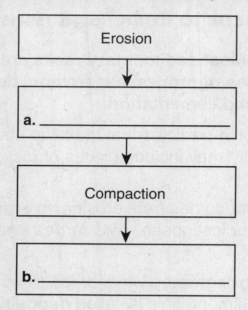

Erosion

a. _____

Compaction

b. _____

Types of Sedimentary Rock (pages 154–155)

Key Concept: **There are three major groups of sedimentary rocks: clastic rocks, organic rocks, and chemical rocks.**

• Sedimentary rocks are classified by the kind of sediments they are made of.

• **Clastic rock** is made of rock particles. The particles can be tiny or huge. Sandstone is clastic rock. Sandstone is made of particles of sand.

• **Organic rock** is made of the remains of plants and animals. "Organic" means alive or once living. Limestone is organic rock. Limestone is made of bones and shells.

• **Chemical rock** is made of dissolved minerals that came out of solution and formed crystals. Rock salt is chemical rock. Rock salt forms when a solution evaporates and leaves behind crystals of halite.

Name _____ Date _____ Class _____

Rocks

Answer the following questions. Use your textbook and the ideas on page 78.

3. Fill in the blanks in the table about kinds of sedimentary rock.

Kinds of Sedimentary Rock	
Kind of Rock	**Kind of Sediment It Contains**
Clastic rock	rock particles
a. _____ _____	remains of plants and animals
b. _____ _____	mineral crystals from solutions

4. Read the words in the box. In each sentence below, fill in one of the words.

sandstone   limestone   halite

a. The kind of sedimentary rock that forms from bones and shells is _____.

b. The kind of sedimentary rock that forms from particles of sand is _____.

Rocks

Uses of Sedimentary Rocks (page 156)

Key Concept: **People have used sedimentary rocks throughout history for many different purposes, including building materials and tools.**

- Flint is a sedimentary rock that was used to make arrowheads for thousands of years. Flint forms when tiny particles of silica settle out of water.

- Sandstone and limestone have been used for the outside walls of buildings for thousands of years. Both rocks are soft enough to cut into blocks.

Answer the following questions. Use your textbook and the ideas above.

5. Read the words in the box. In each sentence below, fill in one of the words.

silica	limestone	flint

a. A rock that was used to make arrowheads is

_____.

b. A rock used to make building blocks is

_____.

6. Why is sandstone useful for the outside walls of buildings? Circle the letter of the correct answer.

a. Sandstone is soft enough to cut into blocks.

b. Sandstone is the hardest kind of rock on Earth.

c. Sandstone forms on Earth's surface, so it is easy to find.

Rocks From Reefs (pages 157–159)

Coral Reefs (page 158)

Key Concept: **When coral animals die, their skeletons remain. More corals build on top of them, gradually forming a coral reef.**

- Coral animals are tiny. They live in the oceans. Coral animals live together in huge groups.

- As coral animals die, their skeletons pile up and grow together. Over time, the skeletons form a **coral reef**. A coral reef may grow to be hundreds of kilometers long.

- Coral animals can live only in warm, shallow water. So coral reefs are found only in tropical oceans near coasts. In the United States, there are coral reefs only off the coasts of southern Florida and Hawaii.

Answer the following questions. Use your textbook and the ideas above.

1. The skeletons of coral animals pile up and grow

   together and form a(an) _____.

2. Circle the letter of each sentence that is true about coral reefs.

   a. Coral reefs are made of animal skeletons.

   b. You can find coral reefs off the coast of every island and continent in the world.

   c. The biggest coral reefs are a few meters long.

Rocks

Limestone From Coral Reefs (page 159)

Key Concept: **Limestone deposits that began as coral reefs provide evidence of how plate motions have changed Earth's surface. These deposits also provide evidence of past environments.**

- A coral reef is a kind of limestone. Remember, limestone is a sedimentary rock. Limestone from coral reefs has been forming in Earth's oceans for more than 400 million years.

- Limestone from ancient coral reefs has been found in midwestern states, such as Illinois and Indiana. The limestone is now far above sea level. The limestone shows that warm seas once covered North America.

Answer the following questions. Use your textbook and the ideas above.

3. Circle the letter of each sentence that is true about coral reefs.
    a. Coral reefs are a kind of limestone.
    b. Coral reefs last for just a few thousand years.
    c. Limestone from some coral reefs is now far above sea level.

4. Is the following sentence true or false? Limestone from coral reefs has been found in Indiana because coral animals used to live on land. _____

Metamorphic Rocks (pages 160–162)

Types of Metamorphic Rocks

(pages 160–161)

Key Concept: Heat and pressure deep beneath Earth's surface can change any rock into metamorphic rock. Geologists classify metamorphic rocks according to the arrangement of the grains that make up the rocks.

- When a rock becomes a metamorphic rock, the pattern of its grains can change. Metamorphic rocks are classified by their grain patterns.

- **Foliated** rocks are metamorphic rocks with their grains lined up in layers. Foliated rocks split into flat pieces. Slate is a foliated rock.

- Nonfoliated rocks are metamorphic rocks with their grains scattered at random. Nonfoliated rocks do not split into flat pieces. Marble is a nonfoliated rock.

Answer the following questions. Use your textbook and the ideas above.

1. Label each circle in the Venn diagram with the type of metamorphic rock it describes.

a. _____   b. _____

     Rock   **Rock**

Grains lined up in layers

Kind of metamorphic rock

Grains scattered at random

Rocks

2. Metamorphic rocks are classified by their

_____ patterns.

Uses of Metamorphic Rock (page 162)

Key Concept: **Certain metamorphic rocks are important materials for building and sculpture.**

- Marble and slate are two of the most useful metamorphic rocks.

- Marble can be cut, carved, and polished. Marble is used for buildings and statues.

- Slate splits easily into flat pieces. Slate is used for floors, roofs, and chalkboards.

Answer the following questions. Use your textbook and the ideas above.

3. Circle the letter of each sentence that is true about marble.
   a. Marble is a kind of sedimentary rock.
   b. Marble is used for buildings.
   c. Marble can be carved.

4. Is the following sentence true or false? Slate is good for chalkboards because it splits easily into flat pieces.

   _____

The Rock Cycle (pages 164–166)

A Cycle of Many Pathways (pages 164–165)

Key Concept: **Forces deep inside Earth and at the surface produce a slow cycle that builds, destroys, and changes the rocks in the crust.**

- The **rock cycle** is a series of processes that change rocks from one kind to another. There are many ways rocks go through the rock cycle. Here is one way rocks go through the rock cycle:

- Igneous rock on the surface is turned into sediment by erosion. The sediment is deposited and slowly becomes sedimentary rock.

- The sedimentary rock is buried by more sediment. Heat and pressure slowly change the sedimentary rock into metamorphic rock.

- The metamorphic rock is forced into the mantle. The metamorphic rock melts to form magma. The magma erupts and cools to form igneous rock again.

Answer the following questions. Use your textbook and the ideas above.

1. Read the words in the box. In each sentence below, fill in one of the words.

   ┌───┐
   │   sedimentary   igneous   metamorphic   │
   └───┘

   a. A rock that melts to form magma will next become a(an) _____ rock.

   b. A rock that is being heated and pressed is on its way to becoming a(an) _____ rock.

Rocks

2. The diagram shows the rock cycle. Fill in each blank in the diagram with the kind of rock that forms.

Rock Cycle

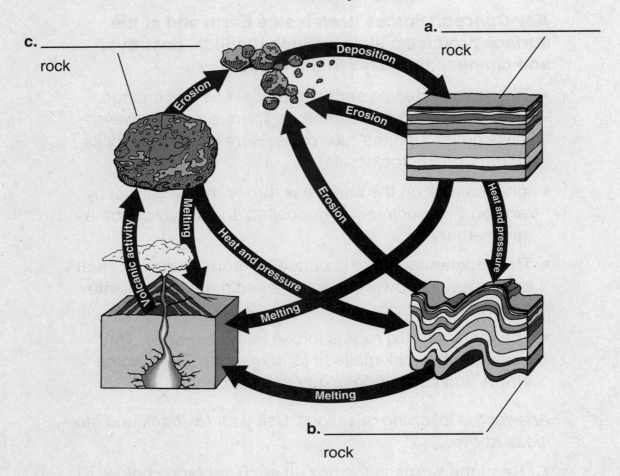

c. _____
rock

a. _____
rock

b. _____
rock

The Rock Cycle and Plate Tectonics

(page 166)

Key Concept: **Plate movements start the rock cycle by helping to form magma, the source of igneous rocks. Plate movements also cause faulting, folding, and other motions of the crust that help to form sedimentary and metamorphic rocks.**

• Two plates may move apart or move together. When two plates move apart, magma may erupt between the two plates and form igneous rock.

Rocks

- Sometimes when two plates move together, one plate sinks into the mantle. Heat and pressure may melt the rock to form magma, which later hardens as igneous rock. Or heat and pressure may turn the rock into metamorphic rock.

- At other times when two plates move together, the edges of the plates crumple. When this happens, rocks are pushed up to form mountains. Mountains slowly wear away to form sediment, which turns into sedimentary rock.

Answer the following question. Use your textbook and the ideas above.

3. Fill in each blank in the flowchart with the kind of rock that forms.

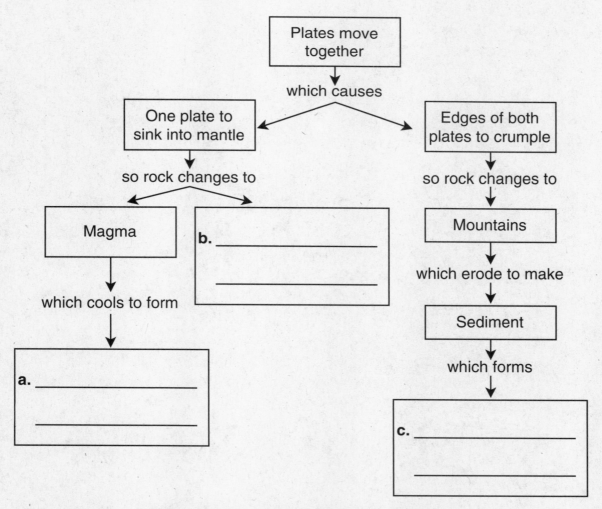